2995

'50s, '60s, & '70s
Kitchen Collectibles

Douglas Congdon-Martin & Tina Skinner

Schiffer Publishing Ltd

4880 Lower Valley Road Atglen, Pennsylvania 19310

Acknowledgements

This book was made possible thanks to the very cool collection and expertise of Dennis and Lori Todd Trishman of Depression Obsessions in Lancaster, PA. They know how to make old look new again, and bring a special eye to their inventory of mid-century kitchen collectibles. Their booths at Mad Hatter Antique Mall in Adamstown, PA and The House at the Village in Strasburg, PA, as well as their exhibits in shows throughout the Northeast, are memorable, and popular, thanks to their unending quest to rescue all kitchen things cool. They can be contacted via trishtodd@aol.com.

A special thank you to the dealers at the Mad Hatter Antique Mall in Adamstown, Pennsylvania, who tolerated our occupation of their lunchroom during photo shoots, most importantly Kristine Landis, mall manager.

Staff people from Schiffer Publishing who put time and love into this project include Lindsey Hamilton, Joshua Stabler, and interns Laura Mikowychok and Kim Hufford.

Copyright © 2007 by Schiffer Publishing, Ltd.
Library of Congress Control Number: 2007928992

Designed by Bruce Waters
Type set in Times New Roman

ISBN: 978-0-7643-2758-2
Printed in China

Published by Schiffer Publishing Ltd.
4880 Lower Valley Road
Atglen, PA 19310
Phone: (610) 593-1777; Fax: (610) 593-2002
E-mail: Info@schifferbooks.com

For the largest selection of fine reference books on this and related subjects, please visit our web site at **www.schifferbooks.com**
We are always looking for people to write books on new and related subjects. If you have an idea for a book please contact us at the above address.

This book may be purchased from the publisher.
Include $3.95 for shipping.
Please try your bookstore first.
You may write for a free catalog.

In Europe, Schiffer books are distributed by
Bushwood Books
6 Marksbury Ave.
Kew Gardens
Surrey TW9 4JF England
Phone: 44 (0) 20 8392-8585; Fax: 44 (0) 20 8392-9876
E-mail: info@bushwoodbooks.co.uk
Website: www.bushwoodbooks.co.uk
Free postage in the U.K., Europe; air mail at cost.

Contents

About the Values in this Book

The prices shown in this book are a fair representation of these items at the time of publication. Prices are based on good to excellent condition, as shown in the quality of items sold by the Trishmans. Prices vary according to location as well, with different colors and styles enjoying varying levels of popularity.

List of Manufacturers, Brands & Designers

Unfortunately, many of the items in this book were not stamped with a manufacturer's name or identifiable brand. The following is a list of manufacturers represented in this book, with short corporate bios. We were not able to find information on all of those represented in the book, and welcome feedback and additional information from our readers to include in future volumes.

Aladdin®

Introducing the Hop-a-long Cassidy lunchbox in 1952, Aladdin® established a name for itself in lunch storage as the first company to send kids off to school toting their favorite cartoon characters. Aladdin® has provided insulated, affordable food container solutions since 1930.

Cressona Works of the Aluminum Company of America (ALCOA)

Designed and built by ALCOA during World War II, the Cressona Works of the Aluminum Company of America (ALCOA) was purchased in the fall of 1977 by Jim Stine, who reopened the facility and made it the aluminum production headquarters it is today.

American Thermos Products, Norwich, Conn.

In 1906, William Walker learned of vaccuum bottle technology in Germany, and just five years later would make the first workman's lunch kit, featuring the now-famous thermos bottle for beverage storage. In 1913, American Thermos Company became Norwich's largest employer, with more than 1,000 workers.

Androck

Founded by Charles Washburn in 1880, the Androck line of kitchenwares is famous for its colorful handles and funky gadgetry, which could be found in kitchens as early as the 1920's.

Anchor Hocking

A leading marketer and manufacturer of glass accessories, beverage holders and servingware, Anchor Hocking was founded in 1905 and has become the second largest supplier of glassware in the United States.

Aunt Jemima®

With such warm campaign slogans as, "Just Like Mommy Makes" and "Nothing Could Be Finer," Aunt Jemima's tradition of making hearty, trusted food and serving products spans 115 years.

Arrowhead of Cleveland, OH

Famous for its Everware line, Arrowhead of Cleveland manufactured what are now treasured vintage kitchen pieces, often numbered to distinguish series.

Ballonoff

Metal canisters, tins and cups were a specialty of American vintage kitchenware company Ballonoff.

Boonton Molding Company, Boonton, N.J.

The molded plastic industry is largely responsible for the development of Boonton, N. J. as a town. Intended to be used as a varnish, Bakelite material made its debut in Boonton, and would be adapted by Richard Sebury in 1907 to make the world's first molded, organic plastic, Boontonware.

Boren Anderson of Denmark

Branchell of St. Louis, MO.

Originally a division of Lenox Plastics, Branchell answered the 1950s plea of American housewives upon the chipping, cracking, and breaking of their household dishes. Thermoplastic dinnerware by Branchell was soon on the tables of most American kitchens, as a both beautiful and durable China-alternative that was also Automatic dishwasher safe.Branchell® It was a leading manufacturer of melamine dinnerware from 1952 until 1958 when it was acquired by Lenox, Inc.

Briggs Shaffner Company

Located in North Carolina from 1965 through 1974, B.S.C. pioneered high strength aluminium products in a foundry process that was cost effective. They developed a line of kitchenwares that was very popular in the United States and abroad.

Brookpark

One of the principal designers during the rise of Melmac (plastic or melamine) dinnerware, Brookpark was a household name and a post-war kitchen staple.

Catherine Holm of Norway

A popular collectors' item, the Catherine Holm bowl and dinnerware line is still sought today for its rare but famous lotus motif among other signature colors and patterns. Enamel strength with classic vintage design make for perfect kitchen pieces.

Colorcraft

Corby's Distilleries, Ltd.

Started by Henry Corby and J.P. Wiser in Canada in the mid 1800s, when whiskey was a part of daily life in Canada. Corby still operates today.

Dansk®

The perfect marriage of style and function, Dansk's simple approach has made them an industry leader for over 50 years. Dishwasher- and microwave-safe, Dansk is synonymous with modern living.

Eagle

Federal Glass

Founded in 1900, in Columbus Ohio, the company began making salt & pepper shakers, goblets, measuring cups and jars for processed foods. By the 1920s Federal was making tableware products, which continued through the '60s.

General Electric

Formed in 1892 with the merger of Thomas Edison's General Electric Company and the Thomson-Houston Company, GE formed an appliance and merchandise department that included kitchen appliances, and today is one of the largest corporations in existence, still with an impressive line of household wares.

Glo-Hill Corporation

Founded in Montreal in 1946 by Sol, Paul, and Leo Globus, and Harry Hill, their lines of popular kitchenware included chrome, glass, and Bakelite.

Heller Hostessware

Featuring 1950s anodyzed aluminum, the Heller Hostessware tumblers, pitchers, and sherbet dishes are still sought today for their practical convenience and vintage charm.

Holt-Howard

The Holt-Howard Company of Stamford, Conneticut was crteated by John and Robert Howard and A. Grant Holt. The company concentrated production on whimsical kitchen items and giftware and is best remembered for Pixieware, produced from about 1958 until the early 1960s.

Kensington

Kilgore, Inc.

Operated in Westerville, Ohio, Kilgore manufactured colorful Shel-glo kitchenware.

King-Seeley of Norwich, Connecticut

In 1960, King-Seeley was able to purchase the three thermos manufacturers from the U. S. , U. K., and Canada. By 1982, the King-Seeley name was replaced by Household International, but the Thermos products made under King-Seeley, such as metal lunchboxes and beverage containers, are still treasured as vintage gems today.

Landers, Frary, and Clark of New Britain, Conn.

Formed in 1862, this company manufactured thousands of diverse products. The company name Universal was adopted in the 1890's for use on household products. The company was acquired by General Dallas Ware Plastics Manufacturing Corp.'s housewares division in 1965.

George Briard, designer

In the early 1960s, designer George Briard was designing modern, experimental shapes for common household porcelain and chinaware. Occasionally commissioned to reinvent entire dinnerware lines, his influence is preserved in many contemporary designs.

Hemco Plastics, U.S.A.

Lincoln

Masterware®

With a huge range of classic stainless steel kitchen items, Masterware® serves up long-lasting and professional-grade products like mixing bowls, strainers, utensils and more.

Mirro

Formed by the merger of Aluminum Manufacturing

Company and the Manitowoc Novelty Company in 1909. The Mirro brand name was established in 1919 for aluminum cookware. The well-known name was modified in 1957 to Mirro Aluminum Company and, finally to Mirro Corporation in 1977. The company was purchased by Newell in 1983, and two years later consolidated with the Foley Company.

National Diecasting
Founded in Chicago in 1937 by Walter Treiber, Sr. and Samuel Gullo, is still in operation today as a third-generation oorganization.

Quality C.M.P. Corp., U.S.A.

Parmaco

Pro-tex

Ransburg of Indianapolis
With a large variety of matching, patterned, hand-decorated kitchen tools and containers, Ransburg's 1930-50s wares are, today, highly collectible.

Revere Copper and Brass, Inc.
Makers of Revere Ware, cookware developed by this company was an alternative to cast iron in the 1930s. The brand's popularity in the ensuing decades began to decline in the early 1960s. The company was acquired in 1988 by Corning Glass Works.

Russel Wright
A leading industrial designer of the 20th Century, Wright's work included all aspects of home furnishings. He created designs for various companies, from dinnerware to furniture.

Rival
Formed in 1932, the Rival Company's first product was the Juice-O-Mat manual citrus juicer, a hit that lasted many years on the market. Later achievements included the introduction of the first electric can opener in the 1950's and the Crock Pot in the 1970's. The company has passed through various corporate hands since the 1960's.

Royalon
Royalon's vintage Melmac bowls and dishes are timeless kitchen collectibles. Often internally divided for extra functionality, Royalon bowls were a popular early 20th century choice.

Royal Sealy of Japan
With exotic designs, such as the Jamaica pattern with its unexpected fruit-and-leaf motif, Royal Sealy of Japan was and is a popular American collectible.

Roymac

Shel-glo Plastic

Sunbeam
Founded in 1897, the Chicago Flexible Shaft Company began to specialize in electrical appliances in 1910. The Sunbeam Mixmaster was introduced in 1930, becoming the company's greatest success. The company changed its name to Sunbeam Corporation after World War II.

Synthetic Plastics Co. of Newark, N.J.

Telechron
Manufacturer of one of the first electromagnetically impulsed pendulum clocks, Telechron patented their technology in 1909 and grew to a large producer of electronic clocks until the 1930's. Today, collectors are still searching for Telechron original rotors and clocks (even non-working ones).

Texas Ware of Plastics Manufacturing Co., Dallas
Just as "Xerox" became the new word for "photocopy," Texas ware became the household term for Melmac dishes, so common was the company's melamine product in American kitchens. Made by the Plastics Manufacting Co. of Dallas, Texas ware is still available today.

Chicago Metallic Gourmetware
Boasting non-stick surfaces, durable components and smart design, Chicago Metallic Gourmetware has always combined the best materials with the latest manufacturing technology.

Watertown Lifetime Ware
Forward-thinking and original since 1946, Watertown has been honored with several design awards, including a permanent spot in the collections of the Museum of Modern Art. With a two-year guarantee against "breaking, cracking, or chipping," you can't go wrong with their signature Lifetime Ware.

Waverly
No matter what houseware you're searching for, Waverly makes it, and makes it well, including a wide variety of kitchen gadgetry and servingware. Sold in leading department stores, the Waverly way is highly-functional, and incredibly stylish.

West Bend
Specializing in cookware, this company's relationships with major retailers such as Sears & Roebuck Company and Gimbel Brothers, cemented the firm's success in the consumer market. In 1968, West Bend merged with Rexall Chemical and Drug, which later became Dart Industries.

West End Pottery Co.

In operation from 1893 to 1938, West End Pottery Co. produced some of the most charming servingware on the vintage circuit today, with semi-porcelain dinnerware featuring intricate, patterned detail.

Western Electric

Introduced by Disneyland's 1958 "House of Tomorrow" exhibit, West Electric's early telephones boasted such firsts as push-button dialing, speakerphone mode, and a door-mounted camera for identifying visitors. Western Electric was truly ahead of its time.

Westinghouse

To rival Edison's General Electric, George Westinghouse set out to establish his Alternate Current (AC) in 1886, which proved more powerful and able to travel longer distances. Westinghouse products could be found in nearly every household by World War II.

Wondermold Industries

Operating from Canada this company created kitchenwares in the '50s and '60s.

Materials shown

Kromex

No mid-century kitchen was without Kromex, a spun aluminum kitchenware material featured in canisters, breadboxes, spice racks and anodized drink ware. Its durability makes it timeless, but the Kromex appeal seems now reserved only for collectors, who still seek a retro look.

Melmac

Melmac is a secondary name for the Melamine compound, a kind of thermoset plastic common in early twentieth century kitchenware and laminate flooring.

Lucite

An acrylic glass developed in 1928, Lucite is often used as an impact-resistant glass alternative for aquariums, hockey rink shields, and motorcycle helmet visors, among other uses.

Bakelite

Bakelite is the brand name for a thermosetting resin developed circa 1909 and used in such diverse products as kitchenware, jewelry, piping, and children's toys. In 1993, Bakelite was designated as an American Chemical Society (ACS) National Historical Chemical Landmark for its significance in the plastic industry.

Chrome

Chrome, a finishing treatment, is made of a chromium coating on many various surfaces, for protection in such arenas as industrial machinery, cookware, and automobiles.

Anodized aluminum

An anodizing finish has made aluminum one of the most popular materials in the modern world. Anodized aluminum is used for spacecraft, for skyscrapers in major cities, and often in residential construction to support window frames, floors, and staircases. And unlike so many contemporary building materials, anodized aluminum is environmentally safe.

Spun aluminum

This term refers to a specific kind of metal fabrication that uses a spinning lathe to produce a harder, thinner aluminum for delicate, cylindrical parts, fixtures, and devices.

Enamelware

With a base of steel, iron or aluminum covered with a glass-like porcelain enamel, enamelware is a strong material that can be subjected to high heat, is unusually even and smooth, and is also rust-proof, resistant to abrasion, and retains a high-gloss true color. Easy to clean and recyclable, it doesn't get much better than enamelware.

Bowls

Medium plastic confetti mixing bowl in burgundy by Boonton ™. $25.

Large plastic confetti mixing bowl, mustard with brown, white, and tan speckles by Texas Ware . $30.

Orange and white enamelware Lotus bowl by Catherine Holm of Norway. $40-50.

Large teal enamelware Lotus bowl by Catherine Holm. $55-65.

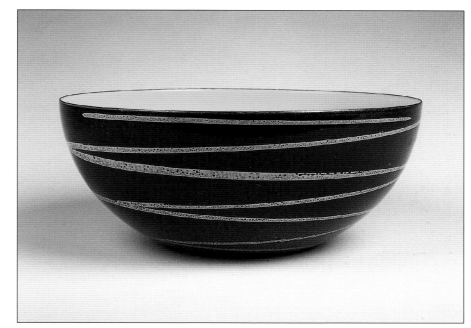

Enamelware bowl. $45-50.

Plastic cereal bowl by Boonton. $8-10.

Plastic lavender serving bowl by Royalon™. $15.

Orange/pink confetti melamine bowls by Boonton of New Jersey. Small $20 Large $30.

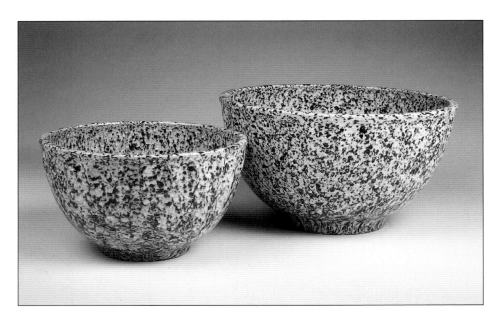

Brown confetti melamine bowls by Boonton of New Jersey. Small $20 Large $30.

Pink confetti melamine bowls by Boonton of New Jersey. Small $20 Large $30.

Blue confetti melamine bowls by Boonton of New Jersey. Small $20 Large $30.

Brookpark plastic confetti medium and large bowls. Medium $20 Large $30.

Two large plastic confetti bowls by Brookpark. $30 each.

Large and small Boonton plastic confetti bowls. Large $30 Small $20.

Two medium plastic confetti bowls by Brookpark. $25 each.

Two medium plastic confetti bowls. Blue bowl unmarked. Brown speckled bowl by Texas Ware Manufacturing Co., Dallas. $25 each.

Large baby blue confetti mixing bowl by Brookpark. $30

Confetti Apolloware medium plastic bowl by Alexander Barna. $25. Medium confetti plastic bowl by Quality C.M.P. Corp., U.S.A. $25.

Two deep salad bowls by Dansk™. $25- $35 each.

Mixed set of large confetti melamine bowls by Boonton of New Jersey. $30 each.

Mixed set of large confetti melamine bowls by Boonton of New Jersey. $30 each.

Set of three nesting plastic confetti mixing bowls in lavender and pink by Brookpark. $75.

Set of three nesting plastic confetti mixing bowls in lime and pink by Brookpark. $75.

Set of three enamelware graduated 1960s mixing bowls with cherries. $40-45.

Three Catherine Holm enamelware lotus bowls. $15-20 each.

Mixed set of small speckled confetti bowls by Boonton of New Jersey. $20 each.

Salad bowl and servers, fashioned in Melmac Colorflyte by Branchell™ of St. Louis, MO. Bowl $20 Servers $15.

Salad bowl with handles, fashioned in Melmac Colorflyte by Branchell™ of St. Louis, MO. $25.

Stackable plastic confetti salad bowls with handles. $30-35.

Salmon, speckled divided vegetable bowl. $15-18.

Plastic bowl by Arrowhead of Cleveland, OH. $18.

Yellow cereal bowls with handles. $5 each.

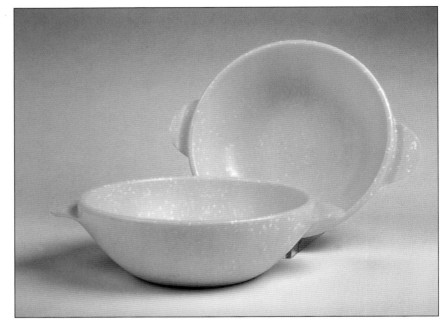

Pink divided plastic bowl by Westinghouse, $15. Lavender divided bowl $15. Melmac Sun Valley yellow bowl, $10.

Boonton turquoise melamine vegatable bowl, $10-15. Divided mint green bowl with tab handles. $10-15.

Set of eight Melmac sauce bowls. $25-30.

Dishes

Five plastic speckled plates in assorted colors. $5-6 each.

Six plastic soup bowls by Hemco Plastics, U.S.A $5-8 each.

Set of eight divided dinner plates in jade green by Dallas Ware
Plastics Manufacturing Corp. $6-8 each.

Enamelware speckled grill plates. $10 each.

Three-piece snack dishes by Westend. $18.

Orange rectangle serving dish. $20.

Set of four stacking wavy dishes. $40-45.

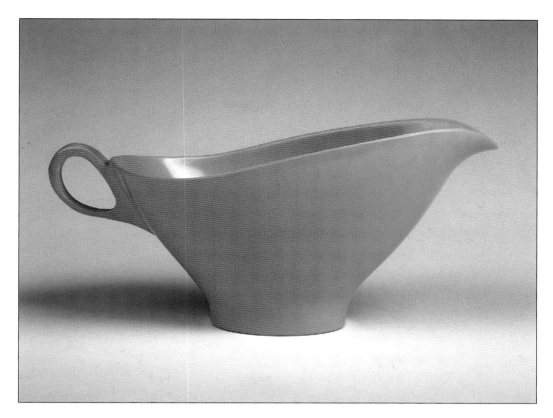

Pink plastic gravy dish. $10.

Dansk enamelware yellow casserole. $35.

Plastic vegetable dishes, fashioned in Melmac Colorflyte by Branchell™ of St. Louis, MO. $20.

Sixteen-piece plastic dinnerware service for four by Roymac in original box. $55-60.

Sixteen-piece plastic dinnerware service for four by Roymac in original box. $55-60.

Sixteen-piece mixed pink and blue plastic dinnerware with plates,
cups and saucers, and small bowls. $48.

Variety of robin's egg speckled plastic dinnerware. Meat platter $12-18, bowl
$8-10, gravy $10-12, cream and sugar $18-20, cups and saucer, $3-5 each.

Sample pieces from a Tropicana 36-piece square plastic dinner service for eight by Brookpark. $95 for eight dinner plates, eight cups and saucers, eight berry bowls, two divided serving bowls, and salt and pepper.

Nine-piece French Chef yellow plastic salad set. $45.

Seven-piece red plastic salad set by Boren Anderson of Denmark. $55.

Twelve-piece plastic oval egg set, six cups and six spoons. $25-30.

Square orange plastic Brookpark dinner plates. Set of eight, $38.

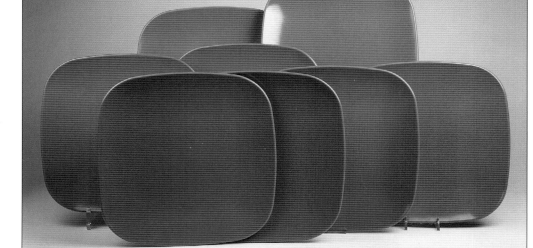

Pink plastic platter, Daileyware by Home Decorations, Inc., Newark, New York State. $18.

Blue plastic platter. $18-20.

Metal enamelware Lotus tray by Catherine Holm. $40-45.

Large yellow floral metal serving tray $18-20.

Pink flamingo tray. $45-50.

Pink flamingo tray. $35-40.

Black and pink tray with fruit design. $15-18.

Set of orange plastic oval plates, Melmac by Boonton Molding Company, Boonton, N.J. $8-10 each.

Plastic confetti tray sets. $30 for 3-piece set. $25 for two.

Plastic trays. Confetti $20. Jade Green $15.

Serving tray and oval dish by Waverly. Tray $40-45. Dish $25-30.

Anodized aluminum Lazy Susan® snack tray, with ice bowl below. $75-85.

Two-piece teak-handled salad set. $20.

Plastic flatware trays.
$15-20.

Glasses

Two glasses with lantern design and gold trim. $18-20.

Set of six frosted rickies, decorated with limes and lemons. $40-45.

Plastic Plas-Tex® glassware. Six-piece set. $35-45.

Black and turquoise glasses, circa 1950s. $38-45.

Eight-piece multi-colored glassware set. $35-40.

Set of six tomato glasses. $28-35.

Nine anodized aluminum tumblers. $5-6 each.

Green and yellow striped iced tea glasses. $35-45.

Six-piece set of iced tea glasses. $45-55.

Set of six multicolored, anodized juice cups by Bascal. $45.

Juice glasses with undersea scene. $5-6 each.

Four of eleven-piece 1950s tumbler set with abstract design. $45-50.

Set of six frosted tumblers in different colors. $30-35.

Set of six glass tumblers in a blue and orange flower pattern. $35-40.

Set of six multicolor '50s glasses $35-40.

Set of six George Briard designer glasses. $45-50.

Set of six geometric design '50s glasses. $40-45.

Cherry tumblers made by Anchor Hocking in a set of six. $40-45.

Set of four tomato juice tumblers. $5 per glass.

Aluminum set of eight multicolored, anodized tumblers by West Bend. $45.

Set of six flared multi-colored, anodized aluminum tumblers. $45.

Aluminum set of seven multi-colored, anodized tumblers
with plastic lids. Lid serves as coaster. $35-40.

Set of eight multi-colored anodized aluminum tumblers with fitted plastic coasters and plastic liners. $65.

Set of eight anodized aluminum soda fountain tumblers. $60-65.

Anchor Hocking polka dot glass tumblers. $25-35.

Soda fountain tumblers in multi-colored anodized aluminum. $8-10 each.

Set of seven mugs with a red brick border and a food and BBQ theme. $35-40.

Yellow pretzels and a black check pattern set of eight mugs (four shown). $55-60 for set.

Set of footed frosted sherbets by West Virginia glass. $35-40.

Set of 4 anodized aluminum footed cocktails in different colors. $40-45.

Set of six glasses by Colony
on a patio carrier. $40-45.

Set of eight tumblers in
a patio carrier. $40-45.

Complete set of turquoise and gold tumblers, shown in carrier. $40-45.

Frosted teal and gold six-piece tumbler set in carrier. $10-15 for rack. $40-45 for glasses.

Plastic tumblers by Branchell ™, $45. Carrier, $10-15.

Set of eight turquoise and white tumblers with "How do you like your drink?"
border and corresponding images in original box. $50-55.

Costumed women adorn these fine blown tumblers by
Federal in original box. $50 for full set.

Russel Wright "Eclipse" designer glasses with one juice, one iced tea, and four beverage glasses.
$20-25 per glass. $10 juice. Iced Tea $25.

Set of tumblers with poker hands on the glasses and coaster/ashtrays. $75-85 for full set.

Set of six multicolored anodized aluminum footed sundae glasses. $55-65.

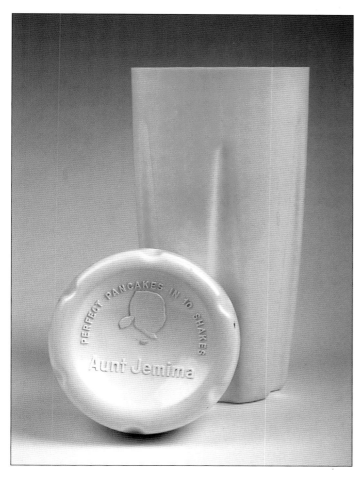

Plastic Aunt Jemima™ shaker that reads, "Perfect pancakes in 10 shakes." $25-30.

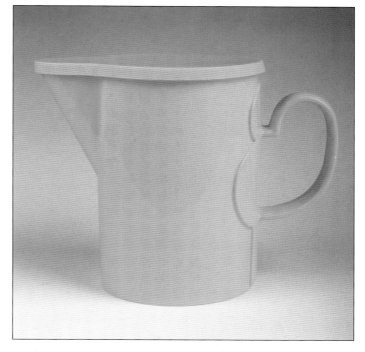

Lidded 1-1/2 quart pitcher with lid by Dansk™. $25-30.

Plastic pitcher by Aladdin ware. $15-20.

Jadite plastic deco ball jug. $35-40.

Plastic orange juice container and tomato juice container. $20-25 each.

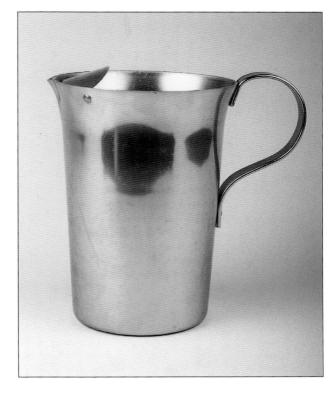

Anodized aluminum pitcher. $30.

Hand painted glass lemonade pitcher. $35.

Small glass pitcher with yellow, red, and blue bubbles. $25-30.

Large red and yellow glass pitcher. $30.

Small orange juice pitcher with orange and blossom design. $20-25.

Large red, green, and yellow circles painted on a glass pitcher. $30-35.

Large fruit pattern pitcher. $30-35.

Small tomato juice pitcher. $25-30.

Small geometric design pitcher $25-30.

Anodized aluminum pitchers. $30 per piece.

Syrup pitcher with red Bakelite handle and top. $35.

Glass syrup pitchers with chrome tops and multi-colored Bakelite handles. Several are by Dripcut. Large pitcher $45. Smaller pitcher $30.

Fourteen-piece plastic pitcher set by
Watertown Lifetime Ware. $65-70

West Virginia Glass frosted beverage set,
pitcher and six tumblers trimmed in gold. $55.

Lemonade pitcher with four of six tumblers shown. $60.

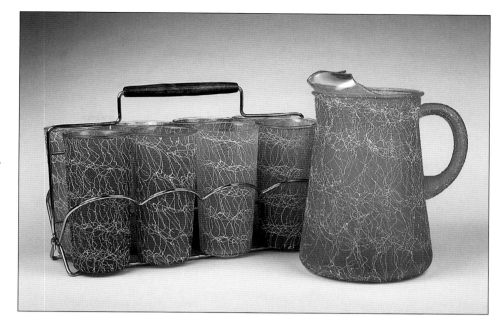

Rubberized, multi-colored iced tea tumblers, shown in carrier with matching pitcher. $68.

Red and gold high ball glasses with pitcher and two ashtrays. $65.

Tomato juice pitcher and juice glasses. $50-55 for full set.

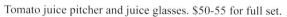

Coffee and Tea

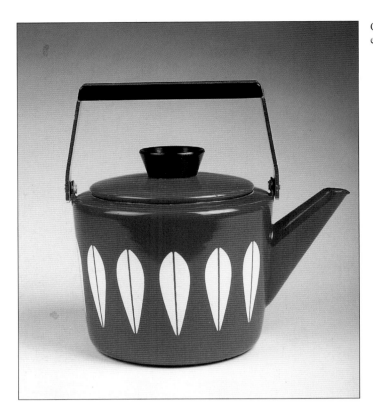

Catherine Holm of Norway red/white Lotus enamelware tea kettle. $65-70.

Catherine Holm of Norway red/white Lotus enamelware coffeepot. $75-80.

Enamelware percolator. $45.

Flavomatic™ blue anodized aluminum eight-cup percolator by West Bend
(cord and box not shown). $68.

Orange enamelware percolator with
vegetable design. $45.

Cookware

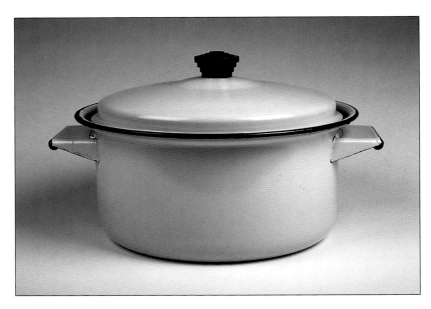

Pink enamelware covered cook pot. $25-30.

Orange enamelware steamer pot. Vegetable design with steamer basket $35-40.

Danish red enamelware quart cooking pot with lid and white flower design. $25-30.

Orange enamelware covered pot. $20.

Black and pink swirled enamelware covered frying pan. $35-40.

Enamelware mushroom-design cookware set including double broiler with egg poacher (not shown), tall pot with steamer basket, frying pan, and covered casserole. $75-95 for set.

Catherine Holm of Norway large yellow lotus covered cook pot. $150. Catherine Holm of Norway Lotus avocado green covered cook pot. $45.

Enamelware Dutch Oven with mushroom design. $35-40.

Pink "Club" Aluminum covered casserole with warmer. $40.

Penguin hot and cold server by West Bend. $40-45.

Enamelware covered cook pot with design. $25-35.

Enamelware U.S. Gourmetware™ five-quart Dutch oven with lid. $45.

Enamelware 2 Quart covered cook pot. $45.

Enamelware Fondue set with mushroom design, $35-40. Set of eight forks, $18.

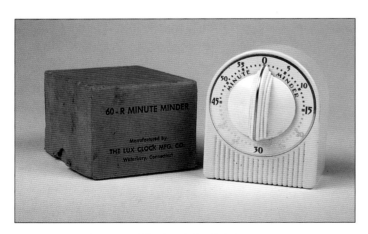

Teak handle stainless steel fondue forks. $20-25.

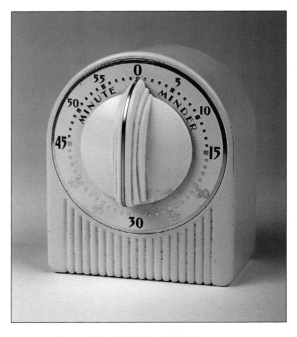

Kitchen timer with original box $25-35.

Resin trivet - lime design by Wondermold Ind., Inc. $10-15.

Litho trivet, 7-inch round. $5-10.

Litho trivet with mushrooms. $10-15.

Resin trivets. Small $20-25. Large $30-35.

Plastic potholder hooks with black-leaf cherries. $30 per pair.

Lemon print towel and mitt set in original package. $20.

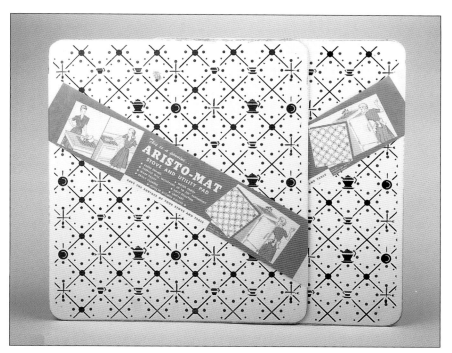

Aristomat stove and utility pads (Asbestos). $25 each.

Aluminum wrapped hot pads by Pro-Tex, one large, two medium. $25.

Spun aluminum grease canister with strainer with copper-tone lid inside. $30-35.

Spun aluminum grease canister with strainer inside by Kromex®. $35.

Spun aluminum cookie canister by Kromex®. $30-35.

LincolnBeautyWare® four-piece square chrome canister set. $40-45

Chrome cookie canister by Eveready®. $30

Spun aluminum four-piece Kromex® canister set. $48.

Kromex® four-piece spun aluminum canister set. $48.

Four-piece canister set in yellow with copper-tone stripe and lid. $40-45.

Set of four plastic canisters in red with ivory lids. $40-45.

Four-piece canister set chrome banded stripes and red knobs. $45-50.

Four-piece canister set in pink and black plastic. $45-50.

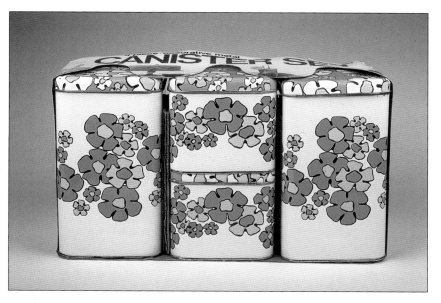

Four-piece decorative metal canister set by Ballonoff in original package. $40-45.

Four-piece canister set by Holt Howard. $40-45.

Four-piece canister set "Chefs" by Parmeco with different expressive eyes on each canister. $50-55.

Set of four round graduated canisters with multi-colored tulip designs and red Bakelite half-disc handles. $55-60.

Four-piece graduated canister set with yellow lids and daisy designs. $40-45.

Four-piece Kromex® spun aluminum canister set with pink plastic lids. $70-80.

Mushroom canister set with orange plastic lids. $40-50.

Four-piece spun aluminum graduated canister set with copper-tone lids and black knobs. $40-45.

Salmon four-piece graduated canister set with trailing vine pattern, by Ransberg of Indianapolis. $40-45.

Green four-piece graduated canister set with hand-painted roosters, by Ransberg of Indianapolis. $45-55.

Pink and gray plastic graduated canister set. $45-55.

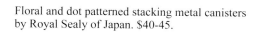
Floral and dot patterned stacking metal canisters by Royal Sealy of Japan. $40-45.

Lincoln BeautyWare four-piece stacking chrome canisters. $45-50.

Four-piece canister by Kromex®. $40-45.

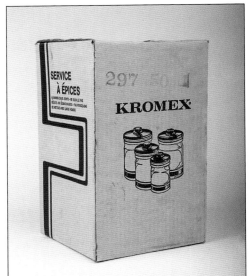

Graduated yellow metal canisters with copper-tone lids, by Ransberg. $45-50.

Kromex® spun aluminum canister set with copper-tone lids. $40-45.

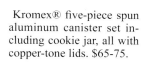

Kromex® five-piece spun aluminum canister set including cookie jar, all with copper-tone lids. $65-75.

Metal canister set with yellow trim and pinecone motif. $40-45.

Four-piece Rubbermaid graduated canister set with floral design on top. $30-35.

Pink and white metal canister set. $40-45

Four-piece Kromex® spun aluminum canister set with Grease and Cookie canisters.
Grease $35, Cookie $30, Full set $50-55. 4 pc. Set.

Five-piece spun aluminum canister set for cookies, flour, sugar, tea and coffee by Hellen Hostessware. $65-75.

Copper-tone spun aluminum stacking Kromex® canisters with grease jar, complete with insert. $75-85.

Orange and yellow laquerware canister set with matching salt and pepper. $40-45.

Five piece pink and gray metal graduated canister set, rice container. $65-75.

Nine piece Kromex® spun aluminum spice set with eight spices in rack. $50-55.

Kromex® spun aluminum and copper-tone kitchen dispenser. $35-40.

Metal wall-mounted dispenser for paper towels, wax paper, foil, and plastic wrap. $35-40.

Metal wall-mounted dispenser for paper towels, wax paper, and foil. $30-35.

Refrigerator boxes in colored anodized aluminum, by Sunburst. $6-8 each.

Stainless steel Revere Ware® food storage set. $40-45.

Morgantown glass mushroom-shaped canister set with metal-finish glass lids. $65-75

Laquerware stacking snack set $25-30.

Laquerware graduated stacking snack set. $25-30.

Bread & Cake Boxes

Kromex® spun aluminum and copper-tone bread box. $40.

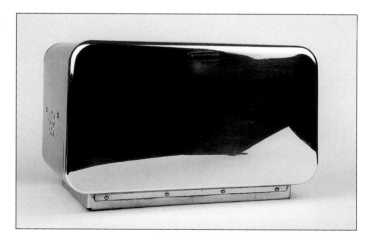

Masterware Breadett™ chrome bread box. $40-45.

"Chefs" by Parmeco® bread boxes shown in two colors. $40-45.

Metal cake saver with chef motif by Parmeco® . $40-45.

Cake saver with glass plate stand and spun
aluminum cover by Kromex®. $35-45.

Aluminum copper-tone flour sifter. $15-18.

Androck Hand-I-Sift® flour sifter with lid. $45.

Spun aluminum flour and sugar range shakers. $35-40 for set.

Appliances

Sunbeam® Mixmaster Junior in original box. $45-50.

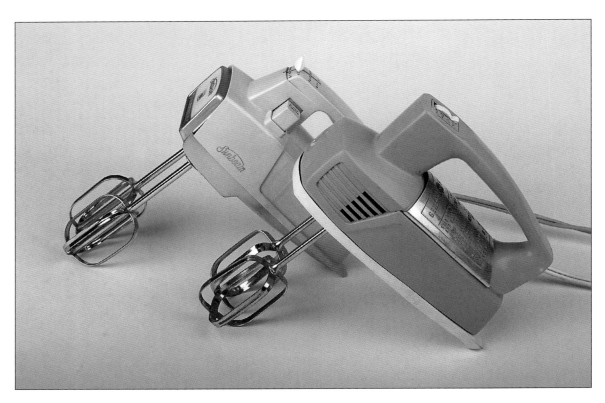

Hand mixers. $35-40.

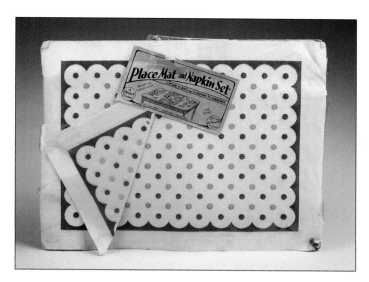

Paper placemat and napkin set with dots. $10.

Paper placemat and napkin set with dots. $10.

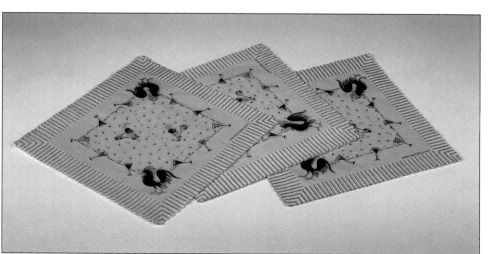

Rice paper party napkins. $18-20 for 30-piece set.

Assorted cocktail napkins, slightly funny and a little risqué. $15.

Resin napkin holders. $20-25.

Plastic wall clocks. $40-45 a piece.

White plastic Telechron wall clock. $50-55.

"Sessions" teapot clock. $48-55.

"Spartacus" red plastic electric clock with black numbers. $45-50.

Metal "Poole" white electric wall clock. $45-50.

Turquoise General Electric® wall-mounted electric clock. $40-45.

Red plastic Telechron clock. $45-50.

Plastic yellow Telechron clock. $45-50.

Emerald green General Electric® wall clock. $50-60.

Electric kitchen wall clock with mixed fruit pattern. $40-45.

Red wall clock.$40-45

Metal wall rack for letters and keys
with rooster design. $25-30.

Resin rooster wall hangings. $18-20 per piece.

Red rotary desk phone by Western Electric with center pin-up embellishment added by dealer. $55-60.

Turquoise rotary dial Trimline™ wall phone by Western Electric, 1965. $55-60.

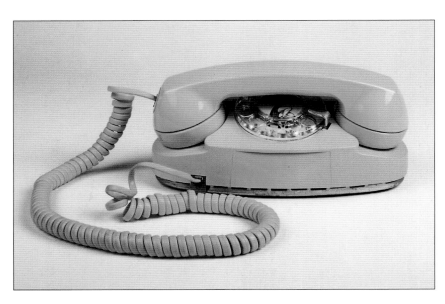

Harvest gold Princess™ phone with pin-up embellishment. $55-60.

Orange touchtone phone by Stromberg Carlson® dated 1979. $75.

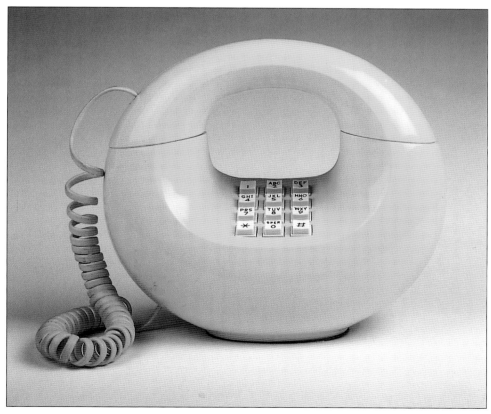

Yellow push button donut-shaped Sculptura phone by Western Electric. $95-110.

Two rotary dial desk phones by ITT in colonial green and orange. $65-70 each.

Two rotary dial desk phones by ITT in beige and gold. $40-45 each.
Tip: Unscrew the mouthpieces on the phones to reveal the date of manufacture!

Trimline rotary dial phones in lime green and orange. $55-80.

Resin flower table decoration. $18-25.

Colorful resin flowers in jug. $10-15.

Resin floral decorations, circa early 1960s. $10-20 each.

Resin flower and owl decorations. $10-20 each.

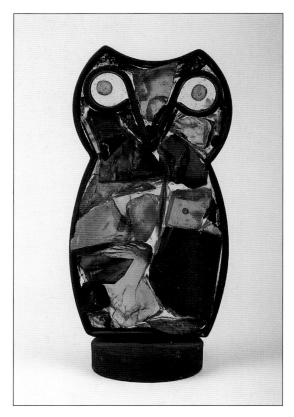

Owl, wrought iron and glass sun catcher. $25-35.

Anodized aluminum candlesticks. $30.

Shakers & Condiments

Plastic salt and pepper shakers in yellow and white. $15.

Chef design shaker set in aluminum. $15-20.

Red plastic deco-style salt and pepper shaker. $30-35.

Copper-tone aluminum salt and pepper shakers by Colorcraft. $15

Bakelite deco style range salt and pepper shakers. $40-45.

Glo-hill 1950s chrome and glass condiment server with Bakelite handles. $95.

Packed Lunch

Lunch box and thermoses, circa 1950s. Red thermos by King Seeley of Norwich, Connecticut. Blue by Landers, Frary, and Clark of New Britain, Conn. Lunchbox by The American Thermos Products, Norwich, Conn. Thermoses $20-25 each. Lunch Box $25-30.

Woven lunch tote and Thermos® by Aladdin. $30-35.

Lithographed insulated picnic cooler. $45-55.

Cocktails

A set of large cocktail glasses and smaller set of tumblers with black and red roosters. Large $6-8 each. Small $4-6 each.

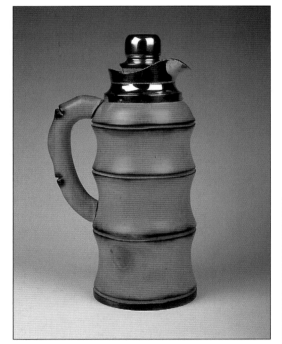

Bamboo cocktail shaker. $75.

Tumblers for Kensington tall cocktail shaker, by Aluminum Company of American Cressona Works. $5 a piece.

Four rooster shot glasses. $15-20.

Shot glasses with "Say When" and pink elephants, "Bottom's Up" and "Here's Mud in Your Eye." $5-8 each.

Pink elephant bar set with six tumblers. $20-25 each. Ice bucket $60-70.

Swinger Party Glass and Chain glass-ware in various colors, shown in blue and gold. $8-10.

Highball glasses, shaker, ice bucket, picks and stirrers. $85-110.

Silhouettes pattern shaker, stirrer, and two tumblers in box. "Mr. Bartender, You, Me, Ours." $60-65.

Set of eight black and white floral glasses and shaker. $75-85.

Six-piece horse-and-carriage shaker and glasses. $75-85.

Six-piece sports theme shaker and glasses set. $55-60.

Sample pieces from forty-four-piece cocktail set with black and red musical instruments. Shaker, ice bucket, six spoons and straws, six shots, six juice, six old-fashioned tumblers, six 4 3/4 inch tumblers, six 5 1/8 inch tumbler included. $295.

Fox hunt cocktail set with six tumblers, six shot glasses, and shaker. $95-110.

Pink elephant set. *A Guide to Pink Elephants Cocktail guide,* $28. Elephant coasters, $10. Elephant shaker, $145. Elephant cocktail glasses, $8-10 each.

Rooster cocktail set, shaker, and six glasses. $95-110.

Four cocktail glasses and shaker, toasting "To Your Health." $55-65.

Coronet Crystal Melody Pattern cocktail set with six glasses, shaker, and box. $75-85.

Ruby red shaker and six ruby and silver striped glasses. Shaker $145. Six glasses $45-55. 4 chrome stem ruby glasses $8-10 each.

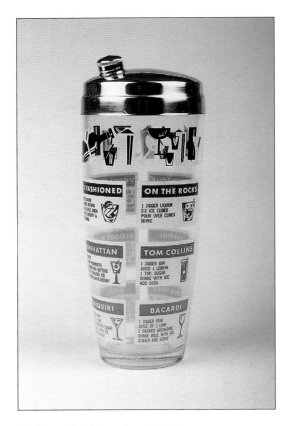

Shaker with drink recipes. $35-45.

Chrome cocktail shaker with white Bakelite ball knob and handle by Keystoneware. $95-110.

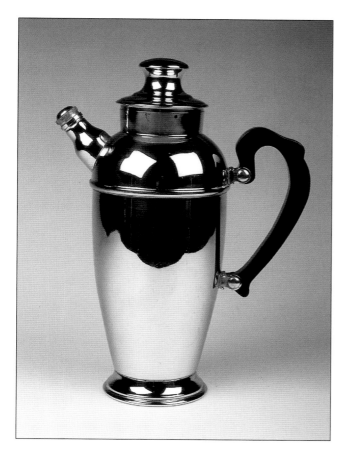

Chrome cocktail shaker with black Bakelite handle. $75-85.

Kensington tall cocktail shaker. $125-145.

Chrome cocktail shaker with red Lucite handle. $55-65.

Chrome cocktail shaker with red Bakelite handle and knob by Keystoneware. $95-110.

Cobalt cocktail shaker with white drink recipes. $125-145.

Gold anodized cocktail shakers by Mirro. $25 each.

Patinel cocktail shaker in stainless steel. $28.

Cocktail shaker with red and black Chinese scene and accents. $35-45.

Cocktail shaker featuring red and white
pattern and chrome top. $35-45.

Recipes in three tones printed on glass cocktail shaker. $40.

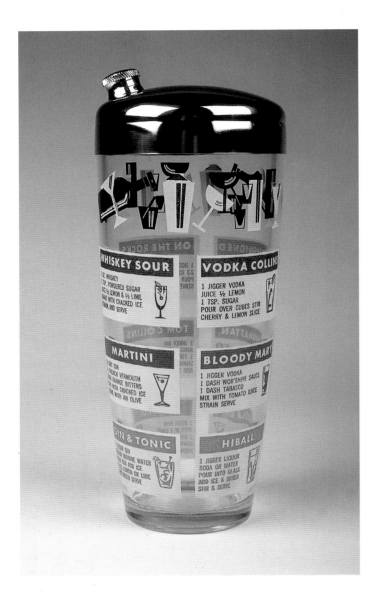

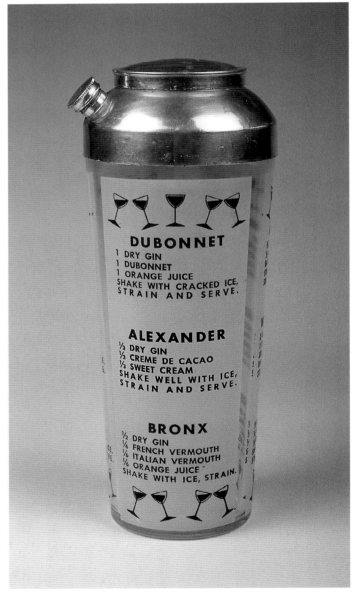

Cocktail shaker with recipes in red and black frosted rectangles. $35-45.

Westbend spun aluminum cocktail shaker with black
Bakelite® top and base. Red knob. $125-140.

Cocktail shaker with drink and recipes. $35-45.

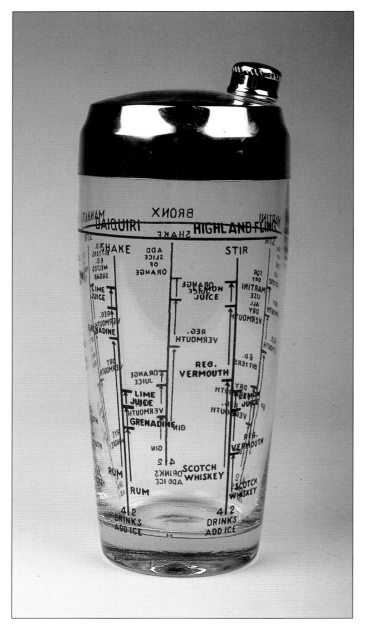

Cocktail shaker with red drink recipes. $35-45.

"Mr. Bartender" shaker with recipes and colorful fruit patterns. $35-45.

Westbend spun aluminum cocktail shaker with black Bakelite top and base and red flared knob. $125-140.

Red aluminum anodized seltzer bottle. $38.

Set of ten tall, multi-colored, anodized aluminum stirs and leaf coasters. (4 shown) $8-10.

Multi-colored aluminum sip stirs from Briggs Shaffner Company, box shown.
These twelve anodized pieces are hard to find. $75-85.

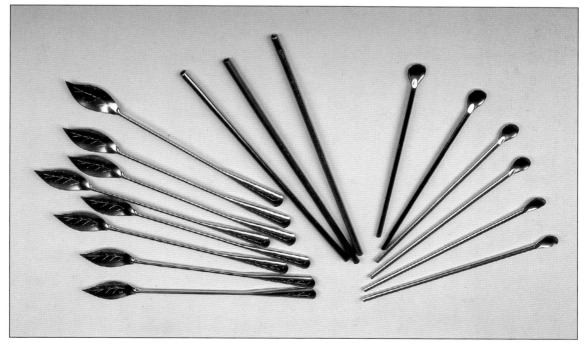

Anodized aluminum multi-colored straws, $25 for set of three. Stir spoons set of six
$20-25. Set of eight gold anodized tall stirrers, $25-30

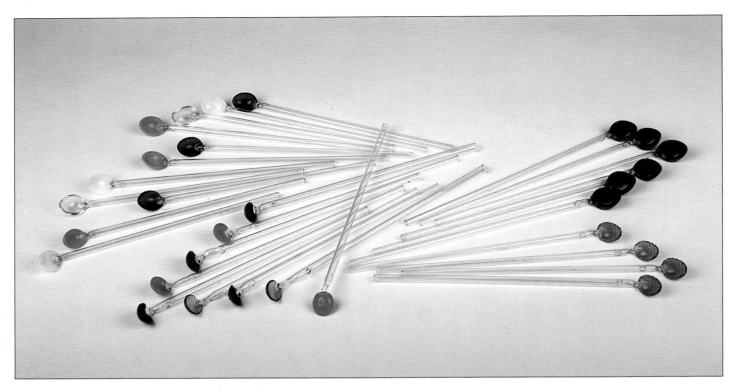

Multi-colored glass straw spoons for sipping and stirring a drink at the same time! Set of six red (top right), $28. Set of nine blue and red with cross at the bottom (bottom left), $40. Set of eleven multi-colored spoons (top left), $50. Set of four dotted green glass (bottom right), $20.

Set of thirteen stirrers with six shamrocks and seven black derbys. $30-35.

Set of six glass muddlers with red tops and bottoms. $25-30.

Set of eight numbered clear glass stirrers. $20-25.

Set of eight glass muddlers. $30-35.

"Spike-Stirs" in box. $30.

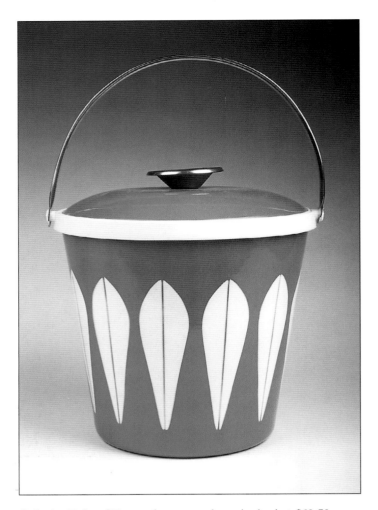

Catherine Holm of Norway lotus enamelware ice bucket. $60-70.

Green anodized aluminum ice bucket with handle and clear knob. $45-50.

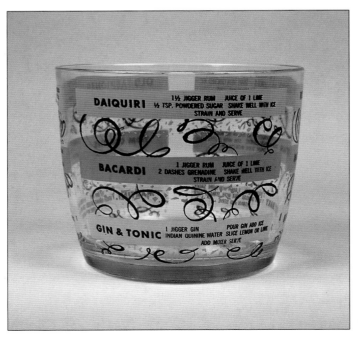

Vintage ice bucket with drink recipes. $30.

Ice bucket with liquor labels. $30-35.

Corby's parrot light $30-35. Corby's light-up, parrot pour spout with original box. $25-30.

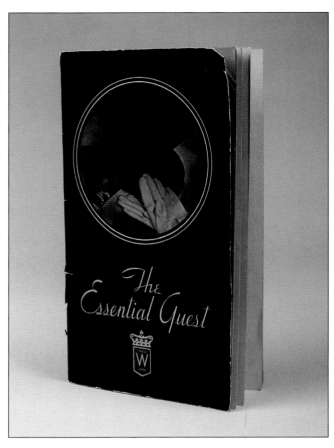

The Essential Guest bar guide by Hiram Walker. $8-10.

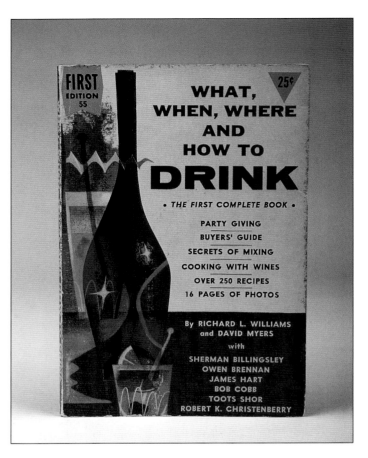

What, When, Where, and How to Drink, by Dell Books. $7.50.

Vintage invitations. $10/pack.

Plastic beverage spoons and coasters. $15-20.

Set of six plastic coasters. $5-10.

Eight drink coasters in "basket" packaging. $15.

"Calories" paper coasters box set. $15-20.

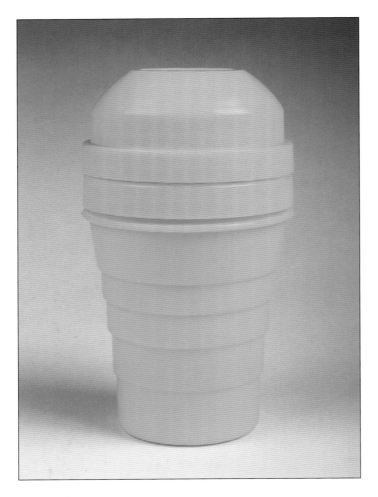

Plastic juicer shaker by Shel-glo Plastic. $15-20.

Juice-O-Mat® in stainless steel. $35-40.

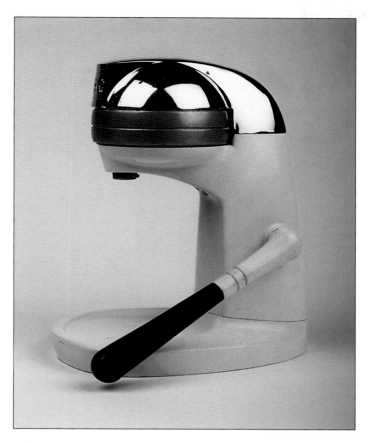

Juice King® juicer by National Diecasting, Chicago. $40-45.

Ice-O-Mat® Ice crusher. $35-40.

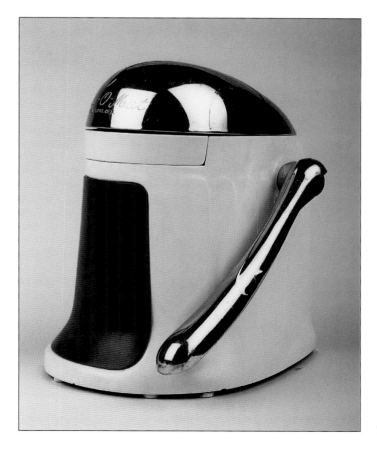

Orange and white tilt-top Juice-O-Mat® by Rival. $40-45.

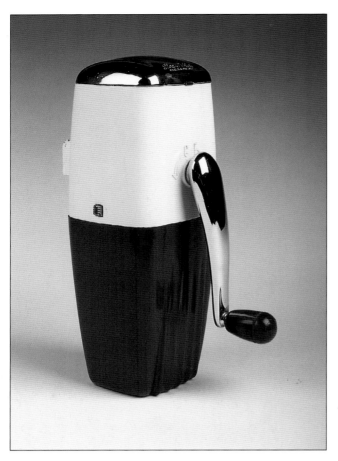

Ice-O-Mat® wall mount ice crusher. $35-40.

Chrome and black Ice-O-Mat® ice crusher by Rival. $35-40.

Chrome Juice-O-Mat®. $35-40

Red and white Ice-O-Mat® ice crusher by Rival. $35-40.

Juice King® chrome juicer by National Diecasting, Chicago. $35-40.

Juice King® chrome and pink juicer by National Diecasting, Chicago. $35-40.

Chrome and turquoise Ice-O-Mat® ice crusher by Rival. $35-40.

Lighters & Ashtrays

Green Lucite pedestal lighter. $45-55.

Lucite lighter with playing cards inside. $40-45.

Blue and white striped Lucite lighter. $65.

Plastic shell ashtrays by Eagle. $8 each.

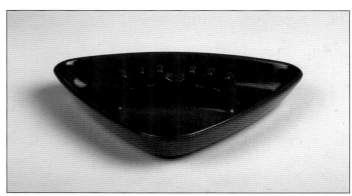

Red plastic triangle ashtray. $8-10.

Plastic triangular ashtray by Eagle. $8.

Black and red plastic ashtrays. $8-10each.

Plastic ashtrays; Triangular speckled tray, $6-8. Round speckled by
Synthetic Plastics Co. of Newark, N.J., $8-10.

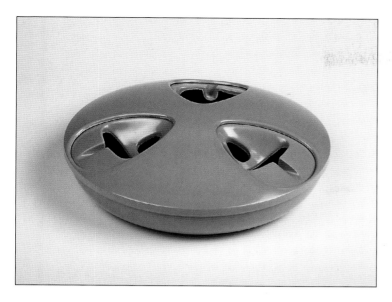
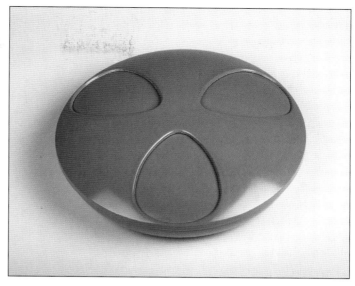

Blue plastic ashtray with three sealing compartments. $20-25.

Magenta anodized aluminum silent butler with Lucite handle. $30-35.

Printed tablecloth. $35-40

Printed tablecloth. $40-45.

Printed dishtowel. $10-15.

Printed tablecloth. $35-40.

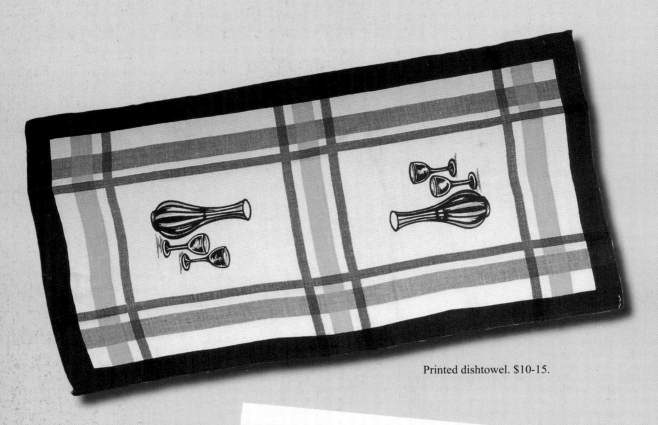

Printed dishtowel. $10-15.

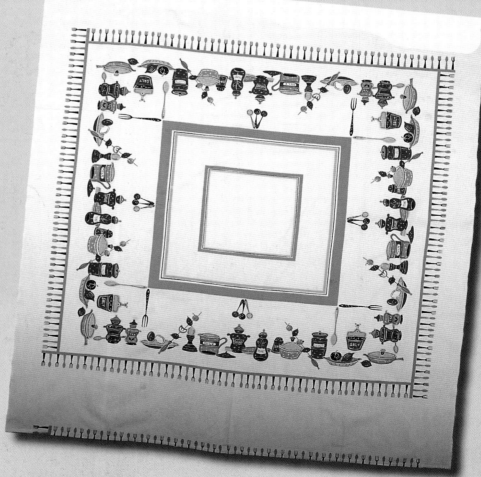

Printed tablecloth. $40-45.

Printed tablecloth. $40-45.

Printed dishtowel. $10-15.

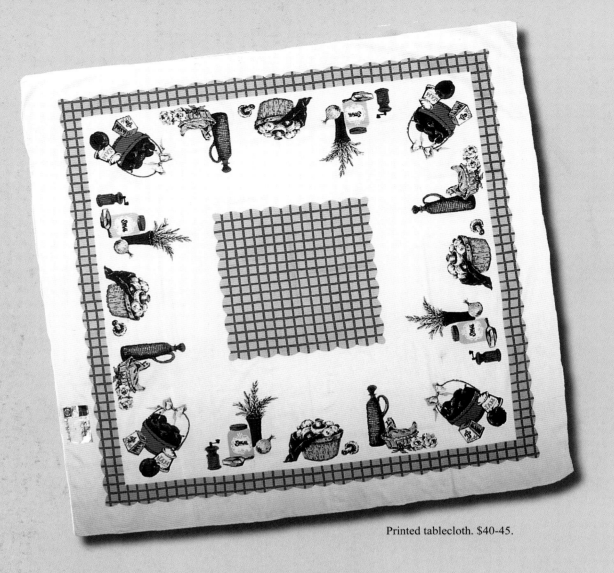

Printed tablecloth. $40-45.

Printed dishtowel. $10-15.

Printed dishtowel. $10-15.

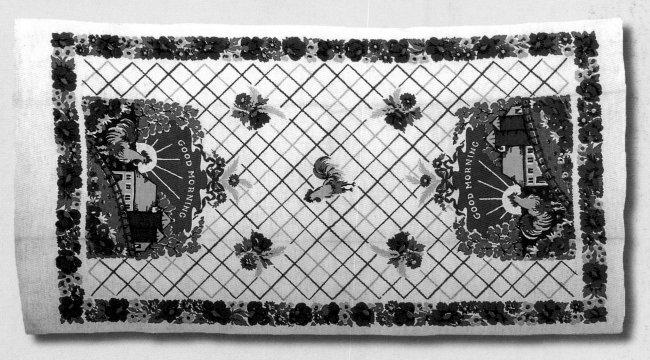

Printed dishtowel. $10-15.

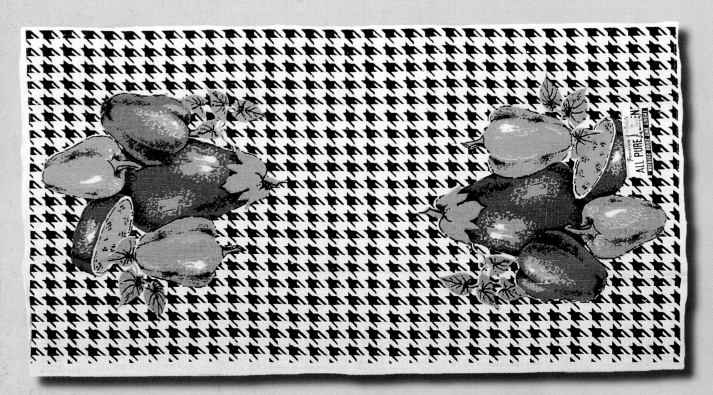

Printed dishtowel. $10-15.

Printed dishtowel. $10-15.

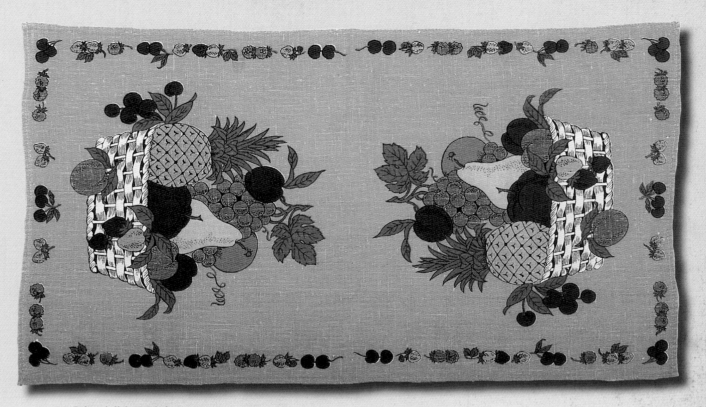

Printed dishtowel. $10-15.

Printed dishtowel. $10-15.

Printed dishtowel. $10-15.

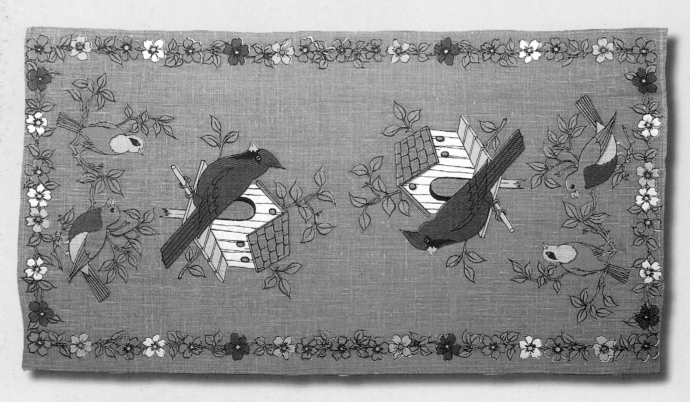

Printed dishtowel. $10-15.

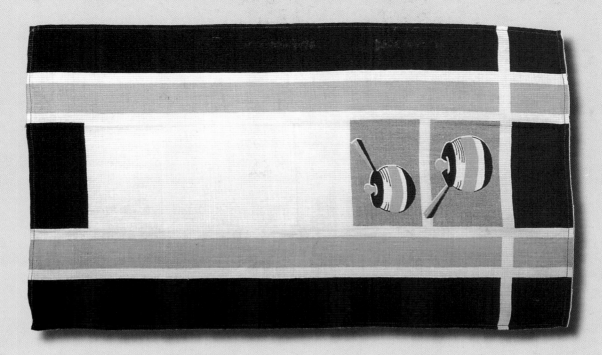

Printed dishtowel. $10-15.

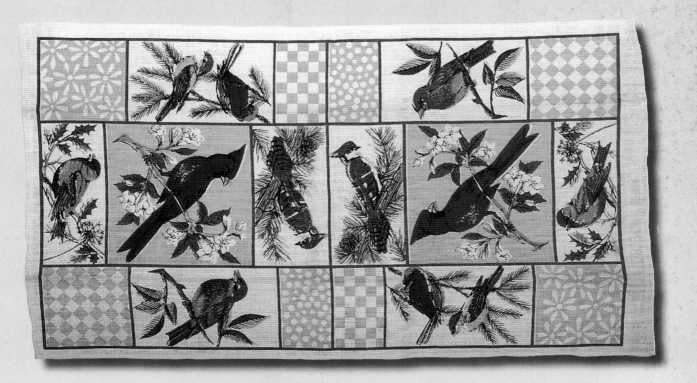

Printed dishtowel. $10-15.

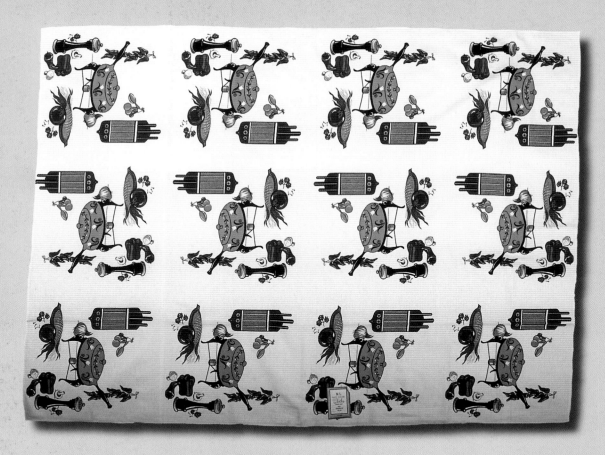

Printed tablecloth. $40-45.

Printed tablecloth. $40-45.

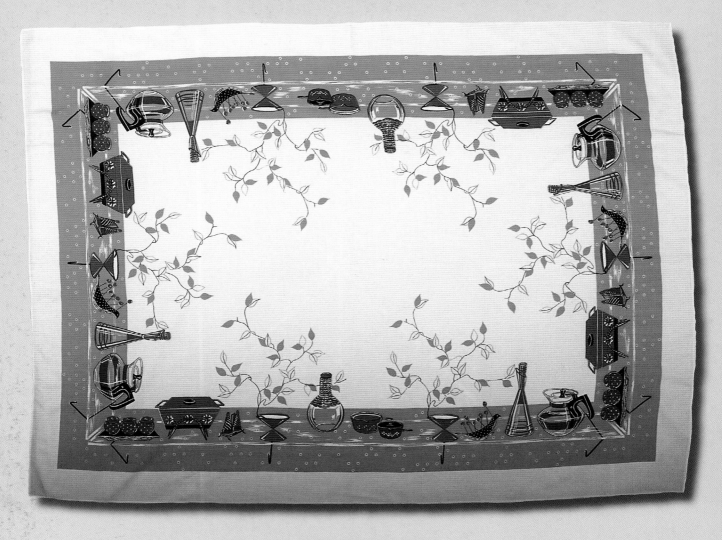

Printed tablecloth. $50-55.

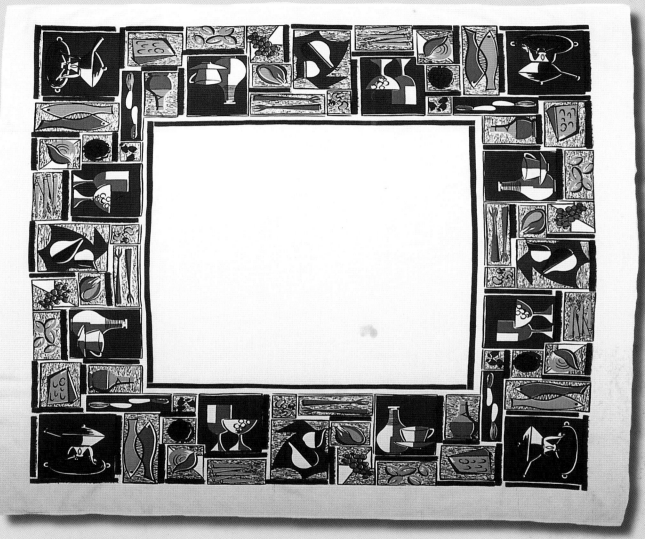

Printed tablecloth. $40-45.

Printed dishtowel. $10-15.

Printed tablecloth. $40-45.

Printed tablecloth. $40-45.

Printed tablecloth. (detail) $40-45.

Bibliography

"Bakelite: The Material of a Thousand Uses." Bakelite Museum Online. Copyright Jurgen Boldt, Berlin 2006. <www.bakelitmuseum.de>

"Enamelware in the Kitchen." Fante's Kitchen Wares Shop. Accessed 15 March 2007. <www.fantes.com>

Goldberg, Michael J. Groovy Kitchen Designs for Collectors: 1935-1965. Atglen, PA. Schiffer Publishing, Ltd. 1996

Keller, Joe and David Ross. Russel Wright: Dinnerware, Pottery & More. Atglen, PA. Schiffer Publishing, Ltd. 2000

"Meet Us." Aladdin (Official Website). Accessed 15 March 2007. www.aladdin-pmi.com/Alad-Meet.aspx

Stine, James M. and Frederick I. Scott. The Cressona Aluminum Story: A feeling of family achieving excellence. Copyright 1997.

Thermos Company Collection. Archives & Special Collections at the Thomas J. Dodd Research Center. Copyright 2002, University of Connecticut.